Limit Of Liability/Disclaimer Of Warranty

The publisher and the Author make no representations or warranties with respect to the accuracy or completeness of the contents of this work and specifically disclaim all warranties of fitness for a particular purpose. This work is sold with the understanding that the Author and Publisher is not engaged in rendering legal,advice-based, or other professional services. If professional assistance is required, the services of a competent professional person should be

The only exception to this clause are Book Samples which are provided for you at various sellers. Also brief quotes may be used in reviews.

So You Wanna Write Urban Fiction

By

Monica Lavelle

Introduction- What Is Urban Fiction?

Please Note: I felt the need to place this statement at the head of this book so there was no confusion on the target market for the contents inside. This book was written for the burgeoning or existing Author wanting to seriously enter the Urban Fiction genre of writing with their eyes wide open. It is not intended to be a guide to teach you how to write. There are already a million books,classes etc.. available to help hone your actual writing skills. This is also not a book intended to bash or belittle anyone currently published or publishing in the Urban Fiction genre. Will this book touch on topics some established Publishers and Authors take offense to? Of course. But they aren't the intended audience for this book either. YOU ARE. This book was created to assist new Authors entering the genre, as well as current Authors who are stumped as to why their work seems to be at a standstill on the various Amazon Urban Fiction charts.

Much of the information inside of this Ebook has been discussed before via various social media platforms. Though for every five Authors who are aware of the various pitfalls, there are twenty new Authors looking for direction. This is for you. The Author struggling to decide if they should sign a publishing deal (Usually and almost always Ebook only.) The Author looking for a Graphic Designer to help bring their vision to life, and the Author who is simply looking for support. Even if it's in the form of this Ebook. I hope that many reading this find the information inside helpful to you. I most certainly would appreciate your honest reviews and believe me when I say, I don't mind the negative feedback. I know it's coming due to the honest, forthright,unbiased information contained within. I thank anyone who takes the time to read and review.

Let's Begin.

So you wanna write Urban Fiction ? Great. This is a genre of fiction that's grown by leaps and bounds over the last 20 or so years. There previously were only a handful of coveted African-American authors writing the gritty tales of life in the " Hood". Now with the explosion of self publishing the need for Authors to submit work to mainstream publishers is no more. Any Author with a story to tell, along with a few tools such as an Editor, Graphic Designer, a computer and an Amazon KDP account can in a matter of hours be a published Author. Now that fact, not statement but fact is a double edged sword. It comes with good and bad but let us not concentrate on the bad. Whether someone writes a good or bad story (You) is honestly up to your readers. I'm of the belief every writer can build a fan base if they're willing to put in the work. So what exactly is Urban Fiction?

Urban Fiction vs. African-American Fiction (What's The Difference?)

Please Note: This section is purely for reference. These definitions were taken from libsucess.org in the event there is someone reading who truly has no idea what Urban/African American Fiction is. If you are familiar with these terms please skip down the page to Authors Notes. *Citations and links will be included at the end of the book.*

Urban fiction, also known as street lit is a literary genre set, as the name implies, in a city landscape; however, the genre is as much defined by the socio-economic realities and culture of its characters as the urban setting. The tone for Urban Fiction is usually dark, focusing on the underside of city living. Profanity, sex, and violence are usually explicit, with the writer not shying away from or watering-down the material.

Also called "street lit", "hip hop fiction", or "ghetto lit", African-American Urban Fiction is a popular genre in public libraries, especially with teens and 20-something patrons. It isn't new -- Iceberg Slim and Donald Goines are two authors who wrote Urban Pulp Fiction during the 1970s -- but there seems to be a renewed interest, perhaps sparked by the popularity of Sister Souljah's "The Coldest Winter Ever". Many of the titles are self-published or offered by small publishers, so it may be difficult to find professional reviews. Street Lit, as opposed to African-American Fiction in general, usually features characters living in inner-city enclaves and involved in drug dealing, gang violence, and/or prostitution for the purposes of street survival or as a misguided means of gaining wealth to move out of the ghetto. This deems the genre as survivalist fiction in dystopia settings. Titles often feature teen protagonists, with plot action containing graphic sex and violence, so the addition of these books to teen areas of the library may be controversial. However, the genre's high appeal to otherwise reluctant readers makes the novels valuable as a way of connecting with young patrons.

Authors Notes :

Even with reading the description above please note, there are some differences in Urban Fiction vs. African-American Fiction. When going the straight African-American route there is no need to litter your pages with slang or curse words. African-American Fiction lends itself more to telling the stories of any other genre (

romance,thriller,mystery/suspense -all

various sub-genres) only the principal

characters are African-American. It should

come as no secret that there are many Black

people who have never stepped foot inside

the ghetto or lived in the projects. The media

at times would like to portray otherwise but

the majority of Black people aren't drug

users or dealers. Most Black people are born

into loving and supportive homes raised by

both parents or a single parents. The negative

aspects of life are all elements that are

prevalent in an Urban Fiction book. So you

have to decide what type of Author you are if

you need a reference here is one. Would you liken your writing to the Urban Fiction Authors Ashley & JaQuavis or Terry McMillan? There is a huge distinction between the works of these three fantastic Authors. Which are you?

Cover Art & Graphic Design

* Disclaimer*

The Author is not responsible for the experience you may have with any of the Graphic Designers mentioned in this book. Your interactions with these designers may vary.

Also please note the advice I'm relaying in regards to covers does not apply to the cover I chose to use for this book! This is not an Urban Fiction book! This is a non-fiction reference book. No frills needed.

Cover art for your Urban Fiction publication is important. No matter how long OR short your book is. Your choice of cover art is the initial element aside from your title that will draw a potential reader to your work. I know trying to self publish your book can be costly; but please don't skimp when it comes to your cover art. In this section I'll provide you with a list of reputable cover designers.

Unless you are a legitimate Graphic Designer, please don't use a cover you made on your project. It screams amateur and cheap. I know, I know, you've been doodling since you were a kid. You draw a pretty good stick figure but save it for your own viewing pleasure. Avid readers are generally collectors of books. In the paperback and e-book form. No reader wants to have YOUR ugly cover displayed in their collection. I've personally seen far too many REALLY good books go unnoticed because of lousy cover art. These very same Authors become angry and disgruntled while they watch let's be honest here...horribly written Urban Fiction books climb the charts surpassing their well written books purely because YOU made the decision to let your cousin who is a genius at using Pic Monkey or Photo Bucket design your cover. Just don't do it.

Speaking of your cousins,relatives or even yourself.

Unless you're willing to pay money for a professional photography shoot, please refrain from using the above mentioned people on the cover of your Urban Fiction cover. VERY RARELY does this go over well. I know you got a 100 likes on your picture. I realize your " Bestie" got 200 double taps on that picture on Instagram. The picture you choose to use for your cover art STILL needs to be of a certain size and quality to be used on your cover art and to print properly for your paperback release.

Please don't misconstrue what I'm saying here.

If you can obtain a quality photograph to submit to your graphic designer for use on your cover art, by all means do it. Every genre...not just Urban Fiction is inundated with a flood covers displaying the same men and women over and over. In the era of self publishing unfortunately it's something that can't be helped. So if you can get original artwork to use for your covers DO IT. Just make sure it's a quality photograph.

Stock Photographs

Stock photos. Can't live with them. Can't live without them. Boy do I wish we could! So let's tackle this topic. I'm sure most of you reading are aware what stock photos are but just in case let me take a moment to clarify in the event there are new Authors totally new to the process. In a nutshell stock photos are pictures sold on various websites for anyone to purchase for their own personal use. Many buy pictures to use in their website designs, brochures etc.. Purchase of the picture of your choice gives you the legal rights to use the picture for various uses including cover art. If you have more extensive needs for the photograph additional licenses may also be purchased. With that being said, please keep in mind that any publishing house large or small, any Author self-published or not has the right to purchase these pictures. I felt the need to remind readers of this and here's why.

You would not believe the numerous

arguments I've read taking place on social media over a stock photo! Authors, we have got to do better. When I tell you these have been out and out battles between Authors that have started on Facebook then extended onto various internet podcasts you wouldn't believe me. But it's true.

Look, I know you feel like you poured over 101 stock photo websites until you felt you discovered the perfect man,woman or couple that represented your book. You gave it to your Graphic Designer and she brought the picture to life. Viola' ! A perfect representation of what you wanted your cover to convey to the reading public. You were so proud of it you put it on your Facebook fan page, you uploaded it as your profile picture. You even had a few faithful supporters change upload it as their profile picture. HOT DAMN! Everyone knows this (man,woman or couple) is on MY upcoming book! You even got 200 likes on the cover art and the comments were rolling in! "When does this drop?", "When is the release date?", "My one-click finger is ready!"

Then low and behold, you look up two days later and see the same (man,woman or couple) is on another Authors book cover!

Oh the outrage!

They "stole" my cover . No they didn't.
They simply liked the same stock photo as
you did. Which they had every right to do if
they so pleased. Let's have a moment of
rational honesty here.

It would be nice if other Authors, especially
those writing in the same genre as you, took
the time to do a little research beforehand. If
they browsed the thousands of Urban Fiction
books up for sale to see just how many times
said photo has already been used but let us

come back to reality here. No one owes you that. Nor does anyone have time for all that. In all actuality MANY Authors do attempt to do this! After all it's not like anyone WANTS to have the same cover art as another Author! Sometimes you can put in the effort for this scenario not to occur and it does anyways. Such is life. Unless you have the funds to pay models for a custom photo shoot to appear on your cover, this is the only and I do mean ONLY way to avoid this happening. Don't sit around angry, just hope your Graphic Designer is a creative soul who can turn a picture most readers have seen 40 times on various covers into a masterpiece for you. Here are a few tips that may help you when choosing stock photos.

I know everyone wants an attractive person on their cover but realize, sellers of stock photos list their pictures on numerous websites. The likelihood of you finding an attractive person you'd like to use for your cover art without others seeing the same picture is slim to none. Stop trying to find the most attractive person you see to use on your cover. After all, in real life, on a scale of 1-10 everyone isn't ranking at a 10. It's okay to choose a girl/boy next door type for your cover. Every female on the cover doesn't have to be wearing a big butt and a smile. Every guy doesn't have to look thugged out.

Play with different concepts for your cover. Every Urban Fiction book doesn't have to display a person at all. What object or scenario can portray your story as well? How can your designer use these concepts to convey an urban setting?

Solicit some of the unknown model websites. You'd be surprised at how many men and women want to BE models but aren't really getting any work. They may have pictures they'd be willing to let you utilize for a nominal fee and credit for the photo. The latest fade I see happening is soliciting friends on social media for their pictures to use on covers. Why not?

Please do not turn to the tactics below out of frustration.

If your book is an Urban Fiction book, where your characters are African-American, please do not use a white woman/man on the cover. (Or the opposite) This is happening all too often in the Urban Fiction genre. To our readers it is misleading and your reviews will reflect this. Imagine purchasing a book with an African-American woman depicted on the cover, only to find you're reading a story about a Caucasian woman (Yes there is a book currently for sell where the Author did this, nor did they indicate it was a Caucasian woman in the synopsis.) don't mislead your readers! There is a plethora of covers in Urban Fiction with depictions of Hispanic and Caucasian women, yet these are supposed to be African-American women? Funny, in these very same books all of a sudden the leading female is Black and Colombian, Black and Puerto-Rican. Come on now y'all. I've also witnessed the most horrible paint jobs on white women in stock photos to make them look like Black women. Please stop it!

Gaudy Covers - Less is more. You don't need to have a thugged out looking man, a woman with her butt checks out, a gun, weed and cocaine all on top of a Maserati. Less is MORE!

Find A Designer

* Disclaimer- In the examples presented, I'm not promoting ANY of these Designers. I simply know for a FACT these designers did in fact design the mentioned covers. This is an accurate representation on their work for any

Author who may choose to work with the Designer. Please Note: Many of these Graphic Designers are also Authors and publishers themselves. Just so you're aware.*

Dynasty Cover Me-

http://www.dynastyscoverme.com/#!covers

Examples- Dark Infidelity by Shawn Starr, When Loving Her Is Wrong 1 & 2 by CoCo Amoure

Great quality, price and delivery time

TSP Creative Inc.-

http://www.tspubcreative.com/

Designer Britney Williams offers a great selection of pre-made cover art as well as custom designs. Visit her website and read it thoroughly. You will need to read the instructions she has laid out for placing a design order and she will give you an indication of your delivery time. Orders are taken via her website.

Examples- <u>Visit this link to view portfolio</u>

Mario Patterson – Find him on Facebook Browse his website and tell him your vision. Be VERY specific with your delivery dates.

Example- Loyalty & Respect 10 Game over

by Drea Delgado

Michah Designs -

http://www.micahdsgns.com/

Example- Visit this link to view portfolio

Titles

In this section we'll discuss the title of your Urban Fiction book. A title alone can draw a reader to your book in the same manner an eye catching piece of cover art can. You want a title that's compelling,intriguing and something that entices a reader to want to know what's inside your book. Now let's address the elephant in the room in Urban

Fiction titles as of late. I'm sure you've seen the plethora of books being released using either curse words or the latest slang terminology. It's rampant, it's annoying to a lot of readers...and it sells.

Sad but true. Many of the main people complaining (READERS) are the ones driving books sales of these titles up the charts. So please don't be fooled by the complainers you come across in the various reading groups who claim " I'd never buy a book with a title like that." , " It's degrading.", " Can't they be more creative than that?" Well of course we Authors could.

But in many cases, why should we when Readers are so eager to 1-click the very same titles they publicly denounce? So let's discuss some of these titles. The main players so to speak.

Bitch Titles

Side Bitch/ Side Chic / Chick Titles - (Which is notoriously misspelled in Urban Fiction. Chic- Pronounced "sheek" is a style of fashion. Chick- (often an offensive term) is a girl or young woman. So the proper title should be written as Side Chick. Even in Urban Fiction please try and use correct terminology!

T.H.O.T Titles- Those Hoes Over There

Hoes/Whores Titles

Thug Titles

Dope Boy Titles

Bae Titles

Nigga Titles

Any song currently on the R& B or Hip Hop charts- (This one is rampant right now. Instead of thinking creatively, you ARE after all supposed to be a writer! Authors are simply borrowing song titles from another creative genre (singer/song writers and taking THEIR song titles.) Some Authors to date are borrowing phrases from songs to use as their book titles (Newsflash- Readers and music listeners are still aware you stole it from a song! I realize you don't care but just to let you know,WE know. We know you didn't use any creativity towards your titles so how much did you use for your actual book?)

This is just a small fraction of terms being used to title books in the Urban Fiction genre right now. Honestly there is no right or wrong answer to this. I'm guilty of using a few of the above mentioned terms myself. It sells. Though in my defense, at the time I used those terms there were a handful of books using them. This isn't a section created tell you not to title your books this way. Just a reminder that it may be wise to use a bit of creativity when choosing a title because as of this writing 2015 any book with the aforementioned phrases is not going to make your book stand out. Everyone is doing it. That can work for you or against you.

Now as a quick exercise, look at the Urban Charts on Amazon.com and check how many of the top 20 books listed are likely to have basically the same title. Small variations but still the same. Go in a different direction. With the over abundance of titles such as these, you need to make your book stand out by showing more creativity!

Elements Of A Good Urban Fiction Story

Urban Fiction tends to lend itself to the same topics and themes over and over. It's all in how you tell the story. So be careful when you're writing so that your story is bringing something new to the genre. Here is a list of common themes in Urban Fiction.

Teen pregnancy

Domestic Abuse

Drug Use

Drug Sales (Also to include cartels,plugs, and connects)

Prostitution

Pimps

Urban Life (Living in the projects and impoverished neighborhoods and communities)

Being a " Ride or Die Chick "

Hood Love & Romance

Love Behind Bars/Prison Life

Cheating/Infidelity

Baby Mama/Daddy Drama

Gang Activity

So now that you've gone through the list, what category does your story fall into? Drug use? Now ask yourself what does your Urban Fiction story on drug use bring to the Readers that they haven't read a hundred times before? Is there a new pitfall your main character will encounter that Readers haven't come across already? These are the questions you need to ask yourself when writing your Urban Fiction novel. I guarantee you Readers have read it all before. Strive to be unique in your story-telling so that you stand out. Now with that being said let me touch on a topic that while not by any means is new and most certainly is not contained to the Urban Fiction genre, it is becoming prevalent. While the readers may not say anything, they DO notice. I'll admit I'm confused as to why Readers aren't calling Authors out for this. I have my ideas but we'll discuss that in the section titled " The Dirty Side Of Urban Fiction". It's the practice of Authors, mostly new, stealing other books and attempting to pass them off as their own. Let me be concise so there is no confusion as to what I'm saying.

There are "Authors" and I'm using the term loosely towards those participating in this practice. Who are making a practice of reading another Authors work then creating their "own" story based off the book they read. In essence re-mixing and spinning a story. Sometimes stealing scene after scene of another Authors book. Taking all the elements an Author used to make their characters different and unique and acting as if they wrote the book. In essence all they've done was change their character names and location and Voila! New book.

Sorry to tell you but avid readers have spotted it. The readers who have noticed are the ones who don't run in cliques, the readers that aren't so hard up for a free .99 book. Believe me when I say those books have been spotted and you ARE being talked about. It doesn't matter if your book is selling and it's sitting with two hundred reviews. You're a fraud and the Readers know it.

Now with that being said let me also state this. Any great idea that's ever entered your mind please know it's not unique. Someone, somewhere in this large, crazy world has had the same great idea as you. But do they have it detail for detail? No. That's the difference. Thieves sneak into an Authors group under the guise of being a "fan" and take a look at all the snippets an Author has shared with their fans and before you know it those sneak peeks have landed in the book of a new Reader turned Author. Sometimes a seasoned Author. For those who don't know let me be the first to tell you. That old saying " Imitation is the highest form of flattery" is complete bullshit. It's not.

Should I Sign An Ebook Publishing Deal?

(What Is That Anyway ?)

Well let's dig into this topic. First let me say this, I have absolutely no issue with any of the Urban Fiction Ebook publishers. None at all. But this book isn't being written for them. Nor is it to advocate for or against them. It's for Authors new and old looking for clarification. So with that being said I will approach this topic no holds barred. Before we start with the pros and cons of signing a deal such as this, let me remind you, these Ebook Publishers have the same tools as you to publish on Amazon. A KDP Account which is free. That's it. Plain and simple. So never feel like they're bringing something to the table you can't provide for yourself. There is only one element an Ebook Publisher brings to the table and that is a fan base. You have to decide if it's worth e-signing on the virtual dotted line.

Pros

Covers - Your Publisher will provide you with an Ebook cover. Please keep in mind, the price you see offered to YOU as an Author trying to purchase a cover from a designer is not the price your publisher pays for cover art. They're buying from the designer in volume so of course whoever they're working with is offering them a huge discount. You may see the custom cover price listed at $100 to purchase it yourself. Your publisher paid between $ 50-60. (Please note: You can find quality covers for less than $100)

Editing - Your Publisher will have your manuscript edited. **Con-** More often than not the editing is horrible. Usually the Editors are no more than readers who have gotten in tight and are cliqued up with a certain Publisher. That's all. No more no less. These "Editors" have no degrees in English,writing, nada, NOTHING. Also let me be more specific. What your book is actually getting is the service of being Proofread for typos and for the amount of typos still found in the majority of these books these "Editors" are doing a horrible job at that. REAL editing is a process that in all actuality takes months to achieve. You read me correct. Months. Real editing is expensive and believe me when I say, there isn't a Urban Ebook publisher out here that is paying thousands of dollars to edit your submission. I'm sorry they're not. And if they tell you they are, you're being bamboozled! What they are doing is paying for your manuscript to be proofread and they're paying no more than $ 150 for that service. I'm being generous with that amount.

Once again, editing is a process that depending on the length of the manuscript takes no less than a month if not months. If your book goes off to the "editor" and your book is loaded and live on Amazon within a week, you've been proofread NOT edited.

Fan Base - I hate to state the obvious but this is the only reason to ever sign an Ebook publishing deal. Period. If you're an Author who has tried your hand at publishing solo and feel that you have a good product (your book). Yet you're having a hard time getting your book in the Kindles of readers this may be the route to go for you. Signing an Ebook publishing deal will automatically get a certain population of readers to buy your books. Readers consisting of mostly women. The owners of most these Urban Fiction publishing companies have their followers for a reason. Throngs of woman readers on Facebook and these publishers play to these women for a reason. We've all all seen them pandering to the female readers on social media.

" Good morning beautiful women!" , " God is good. I stay blessed I wanna give away two Coach purses this month!" , " I want to pay a single mother's light bill this month!", " I sure want a girlfriend. I can't wait for Ms. Right to come along"

You'd be surprised at just how many women act as if they've never been told they were beautiful (Maybe they haven't. Who knows.) The women jumping up to 1-click a book for the slight chance to win an out of date,five seasons old Coach purse. Or the single mother looking at the pink slip placed on her door the day before with her lights about to be cut off. So to be offered a chance to have a bill paid? Who wouldn't jump at the chance? Dammit, I may not have a hundred dollars to pay this light bill, but I DO have.99 to buy this ebook! Maybe I'll win!

There are a few male supporters who chime in every once in awhile but they are few and far between. For the most part none of these Urban Publishing companies even publish men. Each company has a handful or less of male Authors they support in their publishing venture. There's a reason for that.

That's it. Those are the pros. Now on to the cons.

Money – Money of course is a pro but that's obvious and also included in the fan base aspect of signing one of these deals. The majority of the ebook deals offer you a contract with a 50/50 split (This is only if you're signed with the MAIN company. Not a sub-company.) Now I realize some of you may be thinking why is this a con? Well it's a con because there is no negotiating the terms. Say your book is wildly successful. You've completed your series per your contract and have proved you're an asset to the team of writers helping the company grow. Why would you ever settle for getting

50% for the rest of your career? Keep in mind most of these companies don't offer any signing bonuses or incentives. The companies that DO only offer the bonus after your book has been turned in and it's about a $1000 and that's for the series,not per book.

Fan Base- Yes the readers you've garnered by signing with a certain publishing company can be a blessing and a curse. Let me set the scene for you. And if any Reader is offended by me saying this there will be no apologies because as I stated in the beginning of the book. This book wasn't written for the casual reader. The audience

for this book is Authors or future Authors.
So here goes.

If you sign with a publisher the fans you get
through your partnership with that company
are NOT YOUR FANS. Yes, you read
correctly they are NOT your fans. They are
the fans and supporters of the publishing
company you signed with. Now let me also
say this. You may find a small core group of
readers who love your work and will follow
you and your work anywhere you go. But
you should be aware, the majority of the fans
you thought you had,will not follow you
once you decide to leave your respective

publishing camp. That is the reality. I can see the grumbling now from the people who are readers mad because I'm portraying them as a follower. Well I call it like I see it. Sorry. Also keep in mind, if you had followers prior to signing, you may lose some of your core readers. Some readers are adamant that they will not support certain publishers for various reasons. Many of those reasons are justified.

Publishing Camps & Promotion- There are publishing camps who have groups set up on Facebook where book links are being shared and Authors are being pushed to buy books they don't even want to read. You read me correct, Authors are pushed by their Publishers to buy and share. Isn't that for the honest Readers to do? Once a book drops everyone in the publishing camp is expected to automatically purchase. They want you to gift copies of the book to drive up the sales rankings on Amazon. If the book rankings don't reflect sales, people in the group are belittled for not supporting. Now I've been in the game quite some time. Three years ago it was no big deal supporting an Author with a .99 book sale on release day. Now books are being released daily and that .99 per week has morphed into damn near $20 per week.

No that's not an outrageous amount to spend on books per week if you so chose. What is outrageous, is being made to feel you have to spend your money on books you may have absolutely no interest in. You are expected to buy the books being put out no matter what. If you chose not to do so ,you're portrayed as being not " supportive"

No overnight success- I'm throwing this in here as a con only because I've seen a LOT of Authors who have signed Ebook deals become even more jaded after signing an Ebook deal and finding their book still didn't get the traction it needed to be a success. No

I'm not going to put this on the Publisher. As I've stated earlier in the book, maybe your book isn't as good as you thought it was. Also there are certain Authors signed to teams who obvious favoritism is shown towards.

There are Authors on the team that the " fans" will gift copies out. The Publisher will post on their social media that they need THIS particular Ebook to be supported . The Publisher will pay to sponsor posts on social media so that the book is more visible. Well shouldn't you be saying and doing that about each and every release put out? The whole family vibe is put out there but every Author within a company is NOT treated equally and that is a fact.

Sub-Companies- Authors signed to sub-companies get a 60/40 (Author getting 40 % off course.) 30% for the owner of the sub-company and the remaining 30% going to the head of the main company. Now look at that breakdown. It's ridiculous for everyone involved with the exception of the main company owner. You the Author get 40%. The sub-company owner incurs all the costs of running the company. Buying covers,paying for editing etc. gets 30 % . In some of these companies the cost of editing and sometimes purchasing covers may be done by the head of the main company but they're not obligated to do so. The main company owner who has done nothing more than give you permission to use your OWN name behind the word PRESENTS gets 30% for doing absolutely nothing.

Is this publishing or multi-level marketing? What ever it is people are falling for it hook line and sinker. When at the end of the day the only one REALLY making money is the main company owner. In addition to getting 50% off the Authors signed to them, they now are getting 30% from all monies made with each sub-company. Let me tell you something, if all you earn is 30% from being the owner of a sub-company you may need to go to business school instead of writing.

You're not building your own empire. You're building someone else's. Sadly enough many Authors are falling for this because they're too scared to branch off and do it on their own. When you are anyway. Many of these sub-company owners want to grasp on to any connection to the name of the main company and you know why they're grasping? Not because that's what they want to do. They're staying put because by this time they've seen the ins and outs of how these companies work and they're scared to break away.

The whole " losing your fan base syndrome" I'm not the only one to have seen several top Authors with certain Ebook publishers leave...and loudly and publicly at that . Only to come back with their tails tucked between their legs. Because they soon saw the fan base they THOUGHT they had was never really theirs to begin with. And to add salt to an already open wound, they found they weren't always welcomed back with open arms to the fans they previously had.

These very same Publishers love to tout " putting their Authors in a position of power" I call bullshit. Because if that's REALLY what you were doing you wouldn't need to take 30% for doing nothing.

No Real Accounting- When you put your trust in an Ebook Publisher you need to realize that when it comes to monies being made by you, there is no true accounting. On the 15th of the month Amazon releases the numbers made the month before. The only person to actually see the numbers are the person who has access to the account. Do you realize the money is reported in a completely **editable** excel chart? Yes that's right. Oh sure your Publisher may send you the report every month but who told you those are your correct numbers? Some Authors are being robbed blind. The ONLY way you know a true accounting of the sales you made per month is for your publisher to send you a screen shot of the Month To Date Unit Sales. Period. Some publishers aren't even sending their Authors the monthly excel sheets. Where is the transparency? Let me reiterate...**there is no true accounting of**

your monthly sales unless you are viewing a screen shot of the Month To Date Unit sales portion of the Amazon KDP account. Those numbers can not be edited! If you're signed to an ebook Publisher along with the excel sheet they send you, ask them for a screen shot of the Month To Date Unit Sales for the corresponding month. If they refuse to provide you with that. Houston there's a problem. It takes no longer to send than it does to send you the **EDITABLE** excel sheet.

Using Social Media To Sell Your Urban Fiction

There's not much to be said in this section so this will be quick. We're in the year 2015. By all means you need to be plugged into various social media sites.

Twitter,Facebook,Instagram. These are just a few vessels for you to promote your work easily with potential readers all over the world. But please don't forget the old school methods such as book signings in your area and selling paperback face to face (more money for you!)

Please note: It may be in your best interest to create a page just for book promoting use. When you allow readers into your private life via social media you will be judged.

Readers want to connect with you yes but

they don't want to see you cussing folks out

and you turning up necessarily. You must

always remain friendly cordial and always

professional. Also don't bombard readers

with placing links in their inboxes and pages.

Slang In Urban Fiction & Descriptions

noun

1.

**a type of language that consists of words
and phrases that are regarded as very
informal, are more common in speech**

**than writing, and are typically restricted
to a particular context or group of people**

This will be a quick overview of using slang in your Urban Fiction novel. First things first. Just because you're writing an Urban Fiction novel does not mean your use of the English language goes out the window. Sprinkle it through your body of work. It will have more effect for your readers. You also need to realize that readers from all over the United States...the world hopefully, will be reading your book. Every year new slang words are created in different regions. Some of these words become so popular that

they're recognized nation and worldwide.
Those words for the most part are okay to
use in regards to slang.

You the Author needs to know when to
differentiate between regional slang that is
popular in your area and nation wide slang.
If you load your book full of the latest slang
being spoken in Brooklyn, New York (and
even there different words and phrases may
be used in different areas) but a book club in
Houston,Texas has chosen to read your novel
for their book of the month, you may have a
problem in how your book is received.
Readers don't mind telling you via their

reviews they didn't know what the hell you were talking about and rightly so.

This is why I mentioned above " sprinkling" your slang- mainly nationwide throughout your book. Another reason you should use slang sparingly is because you can "date" your book.

If you wrote a book full of the latest slang in 2015, a reader who comes across your book five years from now may not know what you are talking about. That's the beauty of books, they live forever. This is the perfect time for me to address another way a writer can "date" their book. Name dropping the latest clothing designers, and music. I realize you want your release to convey the latest and most popular,coveted items. Just realize when you do this you date your book. It's 2015, all of the designers you've made your character wear everyday will not be what's hot to your new reader in 2016, 2017, or 2018. USE YOUR WRITING SKILLS!

It's perfectly fine to state a name brand design every so often but as a creative thinker, a writer, you should also know how to describe what your character is wearing. You should know how to describe your characters to your readers as well. As a reader I've literally read books where every character was described as a current rapper or singer. Really? In one book the characters looked like the singer Mya, T.I. Chris Brown, Beyonce' and Aaliyh? I've never in life run into so many celebrity doppelgangers. And neither have your readers! Also while I'm at it let me address this as well. If you are a female Author especially, we are diverse and beautiful in every size,shade,weight and height imaginable. Show some creativity in your female character descriptions. I've never read about so many dimpled women in my life! As if that's a prerequisite for a female character in an Urban Fiction novel! The character has deep dimples, long curly hair, a big donkey booty and a flat waist. I know it's fiction but where are all the other women at? Dead?

Now if I ruffled your feathers with that last statement, it must be due to the fact you're an Author and the main female character in your last five books was described just like that. Oh well. You'll get over it. I'm a reader as well as a writer and if I noticed it, dollars to donuts your readers have to. I'm not telling you how to write your characters, what I am suggesting you do is show the world your skills as a creative writer.

Series Or Stand Alone Books

Let us start with discussing the stand alone book. This entire section will be fairly short but I felt the need to address it due to the questions I see about the merits over a standalone versus a series Ad nauseam. You the Author have poured your blood,sweat and tears into penning a title you feel readers will not only like but LOVE. The book is well received, they loved the characters you brought to life in your book and the first review you get states " I hope there is a part two!". In some cases the reader will clearly state they're already waiting for it. Wow! It's just the reception you wanted for your book but it was written as a stand alone book. What should you do?

The choice is yours honestly. As an Author it's well within your rights to turn your book into a series if you feel like there's more to be said, the characters still "speak" to you etc. If a book is good, readers will always want to read more about the characters you've made them fall in love with. As an Author that was your job. When readers request more it's simply your validation that as an Author you did your job. The only thing I would caution you on is knowing when to let it go. Now this what you the Author will have to pay attention too. Here are a few clues that you should let a series bow out gracefully.

Readers tell you to let it go- If after book three of a series your reviews begin to wane, people start to complain that book four added nothing to the series, they accuse you of drawing out simple storylines. You may want to consider letting it go.

Sales Drop- You the Author have lost your passion for the story. Some Authors continue a series because the readers want more but they themselves are ready to move on. If you the Author have lost interest either end the series or wait until you're excited about writing it again. If either of these element are missing your writing will reflect it.

You're accused by your readers of dragging the series out for money. (And you may well be) Many Authors may not want to admit this but it's a valid accusation. I get it. I've seen Authors who have had six or more books out and then on the 7th release BAM! The floodgates open and readers are finally paying attention to your 7th book. You're finally after years of plugging away making some money. So you write parts two and three. Readers still love it...oh and it's still your only book that sells. Like I said, I get it. After all Authors in other genres do it all the time. Just pay attention to the signs of when you may need to leave your series on a high note.

Pen Names Or Real Names

The choice is completely up to you. There are many reasons people chose to write under pen names. They want to maintain their privacy, kids,church or family reasons. Just realize that if you chose to write under a pen name, create a few social media accounts so that you can still promote yourself. Lately Facebook is cracking down on making people use their real names. So keep that in mind.

Pricing Your Urban Fiction Book

The Great Pricing Debate

There's a lot of talk in the Ebook community as a whole on pricing. Not just in the Urban Fiction genre. I'll just try to make this section as fast and helpful as I can. Hopefully I can give you a few pointers in helping you decide what to price your Urban fiction title at.

First things first. You are a Self Publisher. Meaning that you have the right to price your work at any price point within the confines of the platform you're publishing on. Most self-publishing platforms have a minimum selling price of .99 . The naysayers of pricing ebooks at .99 say you're driving the industry down. That readers will expect to read everything for .99. They're correct.

Naysayers say that if you're selling your ebook at .99 you're not making any money. I'll even for the sake of the book go urban on you " These muthafuckas ain't eatin' sellin' these .99 books!" They are in fact incorrect.

VERY INCORRECT. And when I say this please understand that I'm not even factoring in Kindle Unlimited. Pre-Kindle Unlimited, a lot of Authors were making thousands of dollars with the sales of a .99 book. How? Well it's easy. All it takes is having an Urban Fiction title that grasps the readers attention an you've created a virtual money making machine.

In this breakdown we'll use Amazon as an example.

On a .99 priced Ebook Amazon pays a .35 royalty (In SEVERAL forums online I've seen incorrect amounts stated)

So what this means for you the Author is several things. Make sure you've followed all the steps we've discussed in this book! If you can't tick down the list of sections and say you've brought your A-game in regards to your book, that's your fault. It's not the readers, the industry etc. It just means maybe your book wasn't as great as you thought it was. Back to the drawing board.

With a .99 book you need to sell 287 books to make a $100. Seems outrageous doesn't it? All those books just to make a hundred bucks? Absolutely. But don't forget that when you chose to list your book on Amazon you've now published with the largest retailer of Ebooks in the world. Your book is now listed in a store open that's open 24/7. YOU sleep. Amazon doesn't. So once your book gets the traction it needs to be seen, you can sell 287 books every few hours if not hourly. The .99 books you see sitting on the top the of the charts sell that much in volume that yes contrary to what you've been told they ARE making money. Lots of money. The volumes being sold is the very reason they're at the top of the charts.

One of my first .99 books gave me an initial payment of $1,000 and that was with me being signed to an Ebook publisher in a 50/50 contract. I still walked away with $1000 in my pocket for one book on my roster. Now I don't know where you come from,but I pay quite a few bills with $1,000. And bear in mind that was in the first month of release. The book continued to sell.

There are many .99 books that easily gross $5,000 dollars in a months time.

Also what the naysayers also fail to either realize or acknowledge is that in most (usually all) cases, the .99 book is part of a series. There is a method to the madness. I've never understood the uproar in the Urban

Fiction genre over .99 books when if you simply look for yourself, you'd see they are always the 1st part to a pending series.

The .99 book is merely a tool to see how well your book will do. One .99 book can gain you a huge following all while making you a nice bit of cash. If your book is wildly successful with readers you or your publisher will then price accordingly with your part two. If your book was just mildly successful then you'll price at $2.99 - $4.99. If your book has readers screaming for more you'll price higher at $5.99 - $ 9.99 for your parts three,four etc.

Here is my opinion on pricing. I know that often times it seems like you have to follow the pack in order to get sales. I get it. I've watched some Authors play up and down regarding the price of their books. Release day comes and they're amped. Ready to get paid what they feel their book is worth! The book is set at $6.99 and sales slowly trickle in much to their chagrin. Three days later I see the same link only now the book is $3.99. Two days later they're having a " special" and it's .99 . Sigh.

You've caved because no one was buying. Readers like a bargain but please don't get it twisted. They will pay for a book they want to read. Now I'm not going to guarantee that same reader wont buy your book,read it and love the hell out of it. Then return it to buy seven .99 books with the $6.99 they just robbed you for. But a lot of readers are honest and just want to enjoy a good book. Those are the readers you're looking for.

Let me call this to your attention in case you haven't noticed. With the exception of a select few successful New York Times Best-Selling Authors (Not Amazon Best Sellers Chart Authors) none of the Authors in the top 20 have a book that is NOT .99 These are all part one books! The only books that ARE priced higher are part 2's and up! If your book pops on the Urban Fiction charts wonderful ! Outstanding but stop looking at those charts and thinking that any Author NOT on those charts isn't making any money. They are.

Page count – Consider your page count when determining the price of your book. Even though it goes on all day long Authors pouring their blood,sweat and tears into a book only to feel like you have to give it away for .99 . This is yet another reason you can't really knock the pricing structure many ebook publishers follow. The first book is usually one hundred pages or less. Subsequent books are usually longer.

If you're signed with a publisher you wont necessarily have any input on the pricing of your books. That's at their discretion but some Publishers will ask for your input. If you chose to be independent I'd advise you to set the tone for your work. If you put out four releases for .99 and the next book you decide to price at 2.99 some readers WILL defiantly let your book sit there. Readers will try and wear you down until you price according to what they feel like you should be charging them. Think I'm lying? Visit some of the reading groups and observe the conversations. " He wants 3.99 for this book! It needs to be .99 or better yet free!" It's hilarious at times to watch the same reader make these type of complaints and then say " Oh I love to read! I don't mind paying full price for a full novel!" Then of course there's the rant about series which I've already covered.

You dictate your pricing. But you must always be fair to your readers and yourself. You deserve to be paid for your hard work but don't expect to put out a book that is complete garbage and have the audacity to charge $5.99 for your sixty page story.

The Dirty Side Of Urban Fiction

Reader turned Editors – Editing is the most expensive part of publishing a book. I'm not saying you can't find quality people with a strong work ethic willing to PROOFREAD your book. But beware. The book game is a hustle now days and everyone that was a reader before is now an Author,Editor Publisher or Promoter, and Reviewer when five months ago...they were simply reading. Now they all want to get paid. I'm not knocking it. Just be aware.

Spotting a typo does NOT make you an Editor. The readers who are your fans today, next month may be trying to take your fan base because they have a book coming out in a week!

Handling reviews- Contrary to what you may have been told, reviews aren't for you. Yes you can browse them quietly to see if they offer you any input to perfect your craft but honestly most of the reviews done lately look as if they've been left by people who can't even write. It often makes you wonder how they actually read a book. (Don't trip, I said at the start I would be honest.) Do you know who reviews are for? Reviews are for other READERS. Not you. So there should be no earthly reason why you are stalking your Amazon listing for reviews and actually arguing back and forth with any reader who didn't enjoy your book.

Yes Authors actually participate in such nonsense and it's unprofessional. Honestly the amount of HONEST reviews has gone down drastically due to behavior such as this among many other things. So please don't be dissuaded when you see a book from a certain publishing camp with a book that released the day before with 90 reviews.

Believe me when I say, they have been compensated. Free books,advanced copies,Amazon gift cards etc. What do you think the company specific reader groups are for?

Put your acknowledgments at the back- No one cares. Really, they don't. When readers are on Amazon trying to decide if they want to purchase your book, often times they read the look inside or have a sample sent to their Kindles. Don't waste their time having to read your laundry list of people you want to thank. By the time they actually get to the first chapter they get to read two

lines of your book and the sample is over.
Honestly no one cares who you want to
thank. That's an ego thing for you the
Author. Get over yourself and put it in the
back. Anyone really supporting you and
actually reading the book will have a
pleasant surprise when they see their name at
the END of the book!

Email Lists – You should have one. It's the
quickest way to keep readers abreast of
what's going on with you. New releases etc.
If you are independent you should make it a
priority to have an opt-in email list. If you
are signed to a publisher you shouldn't rely

on THEIR email list. Should you decide to part ways once your contract is done, you won't have access to readers who bought your books via those email list. There's no need for me to state a certain provider, Google – Free Email list .

Word Count vs Page Count – Just because a book is 300 pages doesn' t mean it's better than a book that has 150 pages. Readers think the definition of a book is how many pages it contains. Writers/Authors (SHOULD) know it's determined by word count.

Novel – over 40,000 words

Novella- 18,000 to 40,000 words

Novelette – 8,000 to 18,000 words

Short Story- Anything under 8,000 words

Use this as a guide so that you know exactly what you're writing and offering your readers. This will also help you decide on your pricing.

Updated Information w/Kindle Select/Kindle Unlimited – I'm not going to go into depth about these two programs because I feel like you should read the details on Amazon. I will say they're good programs to utilize for sales. I hear a lot of whining about it but the fact is no one is holding a gun to your head to enroll your books in the program. There are many Authors in various genres who don't enroll their books. If you are a new Author it's definitely a tool you don't want to overlook. Honestly the other ebook platforms aren't doing much as far as traffic period. Let alone for Urban Fiction titles. Try it for three months and gauge your own results. I will say this though. If you're selling books for .99 Amazon gives you a royalty payment of .35 per sale. If you book is enrolled in Kindle

Unlimited, you earn as of the last few months between $1.30- 1.40 per sale.

Update- In July 2015 Amazon implemented a new Kindle Unlimited system where in order to really make any money with the program your book not only has to be borrowed but actually read in order for you to be paid. Gone is the day where a reader can borrow your book, flip through a few pages, 10% was all that was previously required and the Author was paid around $1.35 or so. Regardless of the length of the book.

Now Authors are being paid per page. At

this writing October 2015, two months into the program, Authors are earning a mere 0.00058 per page. Less than half a penny. Some Authors are running for the hills. So lets put it all into perspective. If you have a short book that's wildly popular and Readers are reading each page you shouldn't have a problem, your money will be made in volume sold and read not page count.

If you're an Authors who has longer books 300 plus pages, you'll make a killing due to page count along. But your book better damn well be interesting. Some Authors are under the delusion that just because they put out a longer book it's better. Not true. If you put out a long book that a Reader grows bored with after 100 pages you're no better off.

In a nutshell, whatever you write,do it well. In this program any book that is being read will bring in money as long as the book is selling.

Also note- Kindle Unlimited sales are boosting Authors sales rankings but if the Readers aren't actually reading the books, you can have a high ranking ebook that's high on the charts and isn't making any money. Also just as with the old system there are publishing camps trying to scam the system with this as well. Though Amazon is making it harder to do so now which I applaud.

Before certain publishing camps were paying readers to flip past the first 10% of the book so they got paid. It's much harder to entice Readers to do this when they have to flip through an entire book, and stay on each page a certain amount of time (Yes, your Kindles are monitoring your reading behavior).

Who is writing your book? The Readers or You?- Don't let Readers pigeon hole you into either writing more books in a series than you ever wanted to write, or dictate your story to you. Write your book your way. If they want to write a book, let it be their own. Most of them will anyway. One day a Reader can be your biggest fan. The next day they're signed to the same publishing company as you!

Amazon Charts& Rankings- Don't let Amazon rankings rule your life. They change hourly and are easily manipulated. Every time you see an Author posting they want to GIFT a few copies of their book. This is what's REALLY going on. Their Amazon rankings are slipping and their sales are slow. So they attempt to give away free ebooks to boost those rankings up. Let me tell you something, you know how some of these Authors,especially those signed with certain publishing companies dominate the Amazon charts? They GIFT their way to the top. Some have a set amount of dollars set aside with each release in order to gift their way to the top of the Amazon charts. Also let me add, this is not reserved to just those publishing in the urban fiction genre.

Also while we're on the topic of charts. Authors please place your books in the correct categories. There's nothing worse than seeing an Author brag on Facebook about their book being number one and you click over to look and see yeah it's number one...in golf. It's number one in drama and plays, and your book is not a drama nor a play.

Your book should be listed in the appropriate categories. Otherwise your number one looks stupid and irrelevant. Even to YOU. If you don't feel your book is good enough to go head to head with other actual Urban Fiction titles you might as well hang up your hat now.

As I stated before. Don't let those charts

fool you. Who cares about sitting next to a book on a chart that was paid for anyway? It didn't get there because the Readers really chose it. Once again don't let the fact you don't see other Authors on those charts fool you into believing they aren't making money either.

Oh You're Making Movies & Plays And A Sports Bar? - I've seen this lately and it's baffling. So I'm going to make one very valid point then I'm done. Not one of the Urban Fiction Ebook Publishers have EVER had a book released that has made it to the New York Times Best Sellers list or the

USA Today Charts. Now if you're serious about the business of books, shouldn't it be your mission to accomplish that? You haven't reached the top of the publishing world until you can claim that. There is a huge difference between those charts and the Amazon charts. Yes there have been a few Authors who've cracked the 100 plus ranking on Amazon but those Authors have barely made it into the top 100 on Amazon. So what I'm saying is conquer the publishing world and push your Authors to the furthest heights before you dabble in your other ventures.

Please Note: If I'm proven incorrect on the NYT/USA Today charts as of the publish date of this book, I will GLADY correct the information in this book.

Supporters/non supporters- Not everyone will support you as an Author and sadly family is the worst. Deal with it and move on. You can't dwell on people not sharing your links or spreading the word about your books. Find the people that do and concentrate on them. But please remember support goes both ways. If you see someone promote you, ask what you can do in return. Especially if it's another Author.

Are you an Open book- Oddly enough readers LOVE to support Authors who put all their personal business online. The Author who give you a blow by blow of their sometimes pitiful sounding life. Decide if you want to be one of these types of people. It's not my thing but like I said, Readers seem to love it.

The End

Now readers thank you for taking the time to read and I most certainly hope you've found something useful to you. If there are any new developments in the Urban Fiction publishing world I feel YOU need to know, I'll certainly be back! In the meantime look out for my other Non-fiction titles coming soon on various topics. Please leave your review. ~ Monica Lavelle

Citations- <u>What Is Urban Fiction?</u>